THE
CLOUD BOOK

THE
CLOUD BOOK

WORDS AND PICTURES BY

Tomie de Paola

SCHOLASTIC INC.
New York Toronto London Auckland Sydney

for EUNICE H.

ISBN 0-590-08531-X

Copyright © 1975 by Tomie de Paola. This edition is published by Scholastic Inc., 730 Broadway, New York, NY 10003, by arrangement with Holiday House, Inc.

50 49 48 47 46 45 44 43 42 41   4 5 6 7 8 9/0

Printed in the U.S.A.   23

Almost any time you go outside
and look up at the sky,
you can see clouds.

Clouds are little drops of water or ice
hanging in the upper atmosphere
high above the earth.

And if you could hop on a bird
and fly way up, you would see
the whole earth covered with clouds.

There are many different kinds of clouds.
Some are high up, some are in the middle,
and some are low down in the sky.
The three main kinds are called
cirrus, cumulus, and *stratus* clouds.
You can tell them apart by the way they look
and by where they are in the sky.

Cirrus clouds are white and feathery
and they are the highest clouds.
They are sometimes called "mares' tails."

Cumulus clouds are puffy and look like
cauliflowers. They also have flat bottoms.
They are always changing shape
and are low down in the sky.

 THIS IS A CLOUD.   THIS IS A CAULIFLOWER.

Stratus clouds are low, also.
They look like wide blankets of gray
and are sometimes called "high fogs."
Drizzle or snow flurries may fall from them.

There are also many other kinds of clouds.
They have longer names because they
look like cirrus, cumulus, or stratus clouds
mixed together in pairs.

Cirrocumulus clouds are small, fleecy masses
that are hard to see. They are very high up
in the sky. Some people call them "mackerel sky."
The French call them "moutons," which means sheep.

"MOUTONS"

Cirrostratus clouds are high up, too.
They cover the sky in thin, milky-white sheets.
When you look at the sun and moon through them,
you can see a halo. Cirrostratus clouds
are sometimes called "bed-sheet clouds."

Altostratus and *altocumulus* clouds are found
in the middle of the sky.

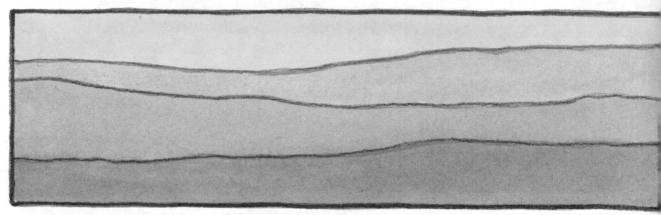

Altostratus clouds look like sheets of gray or blue,
and rain or snow may fall from them.

Altocumulus clouds look like cirrocumulus clouds,
but the puffs are much larger.
They are gray or whitish
and if you walk underneath them,
you might feel some drizzle or snow flurries.

Nimbostratus, stratocumulus, and *cumulonimbus* clouds are low down in the sky.

Steady rain or snow falls from nimbostratus clouds. They are easy to see because they are heavy and dark.

Stratocumulus clouds look like rolls
of blackish or bluish clouds, but
they are not really rain clouds.
They are often seen in the winter.

Cumulonimbus clouds are the kind of clouds
you see during a thunderstorm. They look
like mountains of very tall cumulus clouds.

Fog is a cloud made of water droplets
that form at ground level.
It can come right into your front yard,
especially if you live on a mountain.

Up in the mountains, people give special names to clouds.

One is called the "banner cloud."
Another is called the "boa cloud."

THIS BOA IS NOT A CLOUD. IT IS A SNAKE!

In olden days, people looked at the clouds and saw things.

The Native Americans saw thunderbirds
in dark storm clouds.

The ancient Greeks believed that Hermes, the
messenger of the gods (who was also the wind),
once stole the sun's cattle (which were clouds).

And in Labrador, which is way up north,
people believed that fog was caused by
a white bear who drank too much water and burst.

People saw giants, animals, ships,
and castles in the clouds, too!

There are some sayings about clouds
that help tell about the weather.

FOR FARMERS:

"When the fog goes up the mountain hoppin',
   Then the rain comes down the mountain droppin'."

FOR TRAVELERS:

"Evening red and morning gray
Set the traveler on his way.

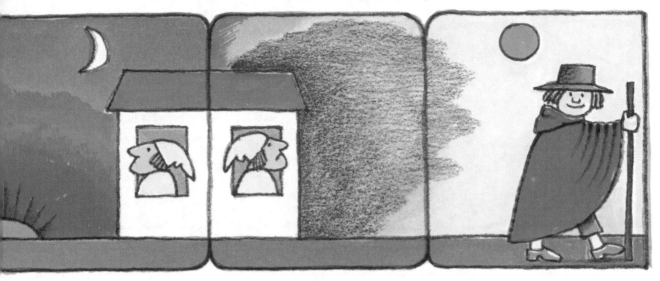

Evening gray and morning red
Bring down rain upon his head."

If there are large clouds in the morning, people sometimes say:

"In the morning, mountains.

In the evening, fountains!"

And sailors know that:

"Mackerel scales and mares' tails

Make lofty ships carry low sails."

There are funny sayings, too.
If people don't seem to know what they are doing,
other people say:

THE CLOUD ENTERS THE ROOM.

THE CLOUD FILLS THE ROOM.

THE CLOUD LEAVES THE ROOM.

THE ROOM.

CLOUD INDEX